Stealth Warriors Arise

OCCUPY UNTIL HE RETURNS

Train – Equip – Activate – Deploy

Dana Carmouche

Unless otherwise indicated, all scriptural quotations are from the New American Standard Version of the Bible.

Scriptures marked (TLB) are from the The Living Bible, copyright © 1971 by Tyndale House Foundation. Used by permission of Tyndale House Publishers Inc., Carol Stream, Illinois 60188.

Scriptures marked (AMP) are from the Amplified New Testament, ©1954, 1958, 1987, by the Lockman Foundation; or are from the Amplified Bible, Old Testament, ©1962, 1964 by Zondervan Publishing House.

Scriptures marked (ESV) are from The ESV® Bible (The Holy Bible, English Standard Version®) copyright © 2001 by Crossway, a publishing ministry of Good News Publishers.

STEALTH WARRIORS ARISE: Occupy Until He Returns

Dana Carmouche
Standard Bearer International Ministries & Stealth Warriors
PO Box 300382 • Houston, TX 77230
Email: dana@sbiministries.org
Web address: www.sbiministries.org

ISBN:9781544831626
Printed in the United States of America
Copyright© 2017 by Dana Carmouche

These strategies are designed to be used interactively as you seek Adonai for revelation and understanding, coupled with the Word of God. No text from this book may be reproduced without written permission from Standard Bearer Intl' Ministries®. These strategies are intended for use as a spiritual building tool and are not intended to supplant your relationship with the Lord nor your responsibility to "study to show yourself approved."

All rights reserved. Reproduction of text in whole or in part without the express written consent of the author is not permitted and is unlawful per the 1976 United States Copyright Act.

THIS PAGE IS INTENTIALLY LEFT BLANKED

This Book is Dedicated to Holy Spirit

And all the Stealth Prayer Warriors that have re-enlisted for

Training-Equipping-Activation & Deployment

THIS PAGE IS INTENTIALLY LEFT BLANKED

CONTENTS

Dedication   i

Introduction   8

1   Session One   Pg. # 10

2   Session Two   Pg. # 23

3   Session Three   Pg. # 35

THIS PAGE IS INTENTIALLY LEFT BLANKED

Introduction

"And he called his ten servants, and delivered them ten pounds, and said unto them, <u>occupy till I come</u>". (*Luke 19:13*)

The charge given in chapter 19th of the book of Luke, is still relevant for the body of Christ today. The Lord instructed us to **occupy** the territory that has been allotted, by maximizing the gifts given until HE returns. Notice that HE called 10, representing [**testimony, law, responsibility, completeness of order, & perfect**]. The greater works should be operating in and through each of us – "Truly, truly, I say to you, he who believes in Me, the works that I do, he will do also; and <u>greater works</u> than these he will do; because I go to the Father. *(John 14:12)*

The earth is waiting in earnest expectation for the sons of God to be manifested. (**Romans 8:19**) God is looking for sons that are trained, equipped, activated and ready for deployment. These sons will rebuild the walls and possess the gates of them that hate them. Like Nehemiah, they will be spiritually responsible for their territory by assessing the damage and strategically designing a plan of action. This manual will serve as a point of reference as each of you replies, "LET'S REBUILD THE WALL".

As I was preparing the material for this manual, the Lord kept speaking NEXT LEVEL in my Spirit. I wasn't sure what HE meant, so I decided to be a disciple of the WORD.

1. Hebrew Meaning of **Next**:
    a. Derived from <u>chayah</u> and it means [alive, living, renewed, vigorous, & flowing]

2. Hebrew Meaning of **Level**:
    a. Derived from <u>yashar</u> and it means [a place free from obstacles, a place of safety-comfort-prosperity, fairness and uprightness in government]

Collectively, the rebuilding of the wall in your territory/region will become a place of safety, comfort and prosperity. The freedom from obstacles will require you to elevate your STANDARD, when the enemy comes in *like* a FLOOD. Possessing the gates of your state, city, community and family will cause living wells to spring up **(Numbers 21:17)**, and revival to come forth.

Death shall no longer be the stench, but instead you shall rebuild and restore:

> "Those from among you will rebuild the ancient ruins; You will raise up the age-old foundations; And you will be called the repairer of the breach, the restorer of the streets in which to dwell. *(Isaiah 58:12)*

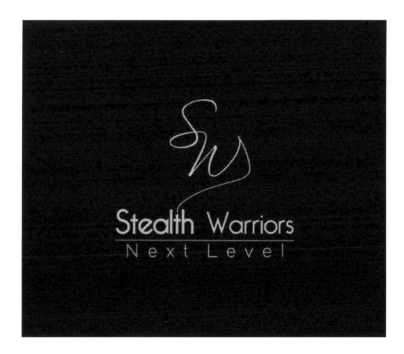

SESSION ONE:
The LORD loves the gates of Zion More than all the other dwelling places of Jacob. *(Psalm 87:2)*

I. GATES

Understanding gates, gatekeepers, watchmen and walls along with their role is very crucial in spiritual warfare. The Lord is looking for trained warriors/intercessors that are equipped with understanding; to deploy the authority of HIS word in the earth realm; thereby hitting the mark. As I have journeyed through life, I've found that I wasn't initially an expert prayer strategist OR consummate warrior, but instead by faith and intercession I have evolved during the process. The tools of my arsenal were battle tested and developed in the fires of life.

The Hebrew word for:
- **GATE** is "Shah'ar"
    - gate (of entrance of palace, royal castle, temple, court of tabernacle)
    - gate (space inside a gate, i.e. marketplace, public meeting place)
    - city, town
    - heaven
- **PRAY** is "Palal"
    - is to intervene, interrupt
    - (Piel) to mediate, judge
    - to intercede *(negotiate, arbitrate, plead)*
- **PRAYER** is "Tefilah"
    - Beseech (request, ask, beg, entreat)
    - House of Prayer
- **INTERCESSION** IS *parga*, which means to
    - **hit the mark** OR the *intended target.*
    - To be effective in your assignment, you must be intentional and specific in your prayers.

Historically the strength or vulnerability of ancient cities was in its gates. Ancient cities were indicative of a fortress because of its colossal stone wall (or walls), coupled with gates that allow or disallow entry of *both* people and animals. The gates are an important part of a territory, not only in its defense but in the public life and economy of the territory. During times of war, opposing forces often focused their attacks at the gates, typically at the weakest part. Therefore, the gates were usually built as part of the defensive guard tower.

> 7 So he said to Judah, "Let us build these cities and surround them with walls, towers, gates and bars [to secure the doors]. The land is still ours because we have sought the Lord our God; we have sought Him [longing for Him with all our heart] and He has given us peace on every side." so they built and prospered.
>
> **(II Chronicles 14:7)**

If the gates of a city are conquered, then the [city, region, territory] was controlled by the conquering nation. Archeologist suggested that the great city Babylon had the strongest and most fortified walls ever built by man. The Euphrates River looped under the outer wall and between the two walls of Babylon. These two-leaved gates of Babylon were thought to be impenetrable, but God has the FINAL say:

> "After these things I saw another angel coming down from heaven, having great authority, and the earth was illumined with his glory. 2 And he cried out with a mighty voice, saying, "Fallen, fallen is Babylon the great! She has become a dwelling place of demons and a prison of every unclean spirit, and a prison of every unclean and hateful bird." *(Rev. 18:1-2)*

The thickness of walls for some fortresses allowed chariots to race on top of them and dwellings to be built within them **(Joshua 2:15).** Rahab's house is described as being in the wall, which is how she was able to let the spies down a rope to return back to Joshua with a report. The fortifications of Jericho were enormous, but fell by the obedience of God's people to HIS Word. The walls of Jericho are said to have stood 45 1/2 feet above ground level. To the inhabitants of Jericho, the Israelites must have appeared to be insignificant and to the Israelites the walls may have seemed impenetrable.

But when God is on your side, no gate can keep you from what has already be allotted to you. The transfer of land and subsequent possession thereof, requires our undivided attention to the instructions that the Lord has given. In **Genesis 12:1-3**, God gave Abram a promise, which included an imperative verb **"go":**

> "Go from your country and your kindred and your father's house to the land that I will show you. And I will make of you a great nation, and I will bless you and make your name great, so that you will be a blessing. I will bless those who bless you, and him who dishonors you I will curse, and in you all the families of the earth shall be blessed." This blessing included land that, at the time the promise was made, belonged to other people." *(Genesis 12:1-3)*

Long before Joshua came on the scene, the promise was in motion to be fulfilled. Because the "earth is the Lord's and the fullness thereof", the whole world and they that dwell therein" (Psalm 24:1), and therefore HE has the authority to do what HE chooses with it. Just as there was a process before the fulfillment of the above scripture, there is a process for each of us to "possess the gates of them that hate us" *(Genesis 22:17).*

> "Whatever the LORD pleases, He does, In heaven and in earth, in the seas and in all deeps". *(Psalm 135:6)*

At the edge of the Promised Land, Moses told the children of Abram, "Do not say in your heart, after the Lord your God has thrust them out before you, 'It is because of my righteousness that the Lord has brought me in to possess this land,' whereas it is because of the wickedness of these nations that the Lord is driving them out before you" *(Deuteronomy 9:4-ESV)* Abram did not inherit the land immediately because the full measure of the Amorites' sin had not been fulfilled, so that judgment could be executed. **Genesis 15:16**, provides us with a better picture of what was seeded into the land, prior to the children of Israel taking possession:

> "And they shall come back here in the fourth generation, for the iniquity of the Amorites is not yet complete."

It was not only the Amorites' but all the inhabitants of the land that God said would be occupied by Abram's seed. The boundaries were established later in the 15th chapter of the book of Genesis, beginning at verse 16:

> On that day the Lord made a covenant with Abram, saying, "To your descendants I have given this land, From the river of Egypt as far as the great river, the river Euphrates: the Kenite and the Kenizzite and the Kadmonite and the Hittite and the Perizzite and the Rephaim and the Amorite and the Canaanite and the Girgashite and the Jebusite."
> *(Genesis 15:16-21)*

The Lord has established boundaries in our lives, and we must adhere to the instructions and occupy the territory that has been allotted to us. In the beginning of creation, God (1) blessed us and (2) gave EACH of us a set of instructions:

> "God blessed them; and God said to them, "Be fruitful and multiply, and fill the earth, and subdue it; and rule over the fish of the sea and over the birds of t-he sky and over every living thing that moves on the earth."
> **(Genesis 1:28)**

In order to be more effective within our boundaries and occupy our territory, we must understand gates. A <u>gate</u> is a **seat of authority** and speaks of boundary markers or barriers and its power *or* limit of influence.

1. Hebrew meaning of **Gate**:
   a. Shah'ar which means:
      i. An opening, a door, or an entrance:

2. Jesus states in **John 14:6**: "I am the way, the truth, and the life, no one comes to the Father but through me."

3. **John 10:9** says, "I am the door; if anyone enters through me, he shall be saved, and go in and out, and find pasture."

4. **Luke 11:9** - "So I say to you, ask, and it will be given to you; seek, and you will find; knock, and the door will be opened to you."

5. **2 Samuel 19:8** – So the king arose and sat in the gate. When they told all the people, saying, "Behold, the king is sitting in the gate," then all the people came before the king.

6. **Psalm 24:7** – "Lift up your heads, O gates, And be lifted up, O ancient doors, That the King of glory may come in!"
   a. This verses gives insight to the conquered kingdom of Satan as the Lord Jesus Christ approaches to bring all the souls out,
   b. **Colossians 2:15** – "When He had <u>disarmed the rulers and authorities,</u> He made a public display of them, having triumphed over them through Him."
   c. **Luke 9:1** – "And He called the twelve together, and gave them *power and authority* over all the demons and to heal diseases."
   d. **Revelation 1:18** – "I am the First and the Last, the living One; and I was dead, and behold, I am alive forevermore, and I have the **keys of death and of Hades**."
   e. *Isaiah 5:14* Therefore Sheol (the realm of the dead) has increased its appetite and opened its mouth beyond measure; And [a]Jerusalem's splendor, her multitude, her [boisterous] uproar and her [drunken] revelers descend into it.

f. **Matthew 16:18** - "I also say to you that you are Peter, and upon this rock I will build My church; and the **gates of Hades** *will not* overpower it."
   i. The gates of Hades/Sheol is a boundary marker indicating the limits of Hell, and it's influence.
g. **Hebrews 10:10** – By this will we have been *sanctified through the offering* of the **body of Jesus Christ** once for all.

7. **Matthew 7:13-14** - "Enter through the narrow gate; for the gate is wide and the way is broad that leads to destruction, and there are many who enter through it. 14 For the gate is small and the way is narrow that leads to life, and there are few who find it.
   a. **Proverbs 14:12** – "There is a way which seems right to a man, But its end is the way of death."

8. **Isaiah 62:10-12** - "Go through, go through the gates, Clear the way for the people; Build up, build up the highway, Remove the stones, lift up a standard over the peoples. Behold, the Lord has proclaimed to the end of the earth, Say to the daughter of Zion, "Lo, your salvation comes; Behold His reward is with Him, and His recompense before Him." And they will call them, "The holy people, redeemed of the Lord"; And you will be called, "Sought out, a **city not forsaken**."
   a. The tone used in the opening of this scripture is an imperative tone. The word **"go"** is an imperative verb.
      i. An imperative verb is used to (1) give orders, (2) commands, (3) warning or (4) instructions.
      ii. As we go through the gates, we are to clear the way for people
         1. Isaiah 62:6-7 – "On your walls, O Jerusalem, I have appointed watchmen; All day and all night they will never keep silent. You who remind the LORD, take no rest for yourselves; 7And give Him no rest until He establishes And makes Jerusalem a praise in the earth."
         2. Our prayers will clear the way for those persons that do not know the Lord Jesus as their personal savior.

iii. Build up the highway
   1. **Mark 1:2-4** - As it is written in Isaiah the prophet: "Behold, I send My messenger ahead of You, Who will prepare Your way; the voice of one crying in the wilderness, 'Make ready the way of the Lord, Make His paths straight. John the Baptist appeared in the wilderness preaching a baptism of repentance for the forgiveness of sins."
      a. We are to create an access that is unhindered and free from obstacles, allowing us to move swiftly.

iv. Remove the stones
   1. **Ezekiel 36:26** - "Moreover I will give you a new heart and put a new spirit within you. I will remove the heart of stone from your flesh and give you a heart of flesh."
      a. Do not let a stone of offense, hatred, jealousy, envy, discord, etc., be a stumbling block.

v. We are likened **to a city** that will not be forsaken.
   1. **Matthew 5:14, 16 -** "You are the light of the world. A city set on a hill cannot be hidden..." "Let your light shine before men in such a way that they may see your good works, and glorify your Father who is in heaven."

MATE SCRIPTURE

9. **Isaiah 40:3-5** - A voice is calling, "Clear the way for the LORD in the wilderness; Make smooth in the desert a highway for our God. "Let every valley be lifted up, And every mountain and hill be made low; And let the rough ground become a plain, And the rugged terrain a broad valley; <u>Then the glory of the LORD</u> will be revealed, And all flesh will see it together; For the mouth of the LORD has spoken."

   a. **Deuteronomy 19:15b** - on the evidence of two or three witnesses a matter shall be confirmed.
      i. As we clear the way, remove the stones and build a highway, THEN the Glory of the Lord will be REVEALED!

II. WHERE ARE GATES FOUND?

1. City Entrance
    a. **Genesis 19:1** – "The two angels arrived at Sodom in the evening, and Lot was sitting in the **gateway of the city.** When he saw them, he got up to meet them and bowed down with his face to the ground."
    b. **Judges 16:3** - "But Samson lay there only until the middle of the night. Then he got up and took hold of the doors of the **city gate**, together with the two posts, and tore them loose, bar and all. He lifted them to his shoulders and carried them to the top of the hill that faces Hebron."

2. Town/Tent/Camp
    a. **Lamentations 5:14** - Elders are gone from the gate, Young men from their music.
    b. **Nehemiah 1:3** - They said to me, "The remnant there in the province who survived the captivity are in great distress and reproach, and the wall of Jerusalem is broken down and its gates are burned with fire."
    c. Exodus 32:25-26 – "Now when Moses saw that the people were out of control, for Aaron had let them get out of control to be a derision among their enemies – then Moses stood in the gate of the camp, and said, Whoever is for the Lord, come to me!"

3. Public meeting place
    a. **Genesis 34:20** – "So Hamor and his son Shechem came to the gate of their city and spoke to the men of their city, saying…"
    b. **Genesis 23:10** – "Now Ephron was sitting among the sons of Heth; and Ephron the Hittite answered Abraham in the hearing of the sons of Heth; even of all who went in at the gate of his city, saying…"

4. Marketplace
    a. **2 Kings 7:1** – "Then Elisha said, "Listen to the word of the LORD; thus says the LORD, 'Tomorrow about this time a measure of fine flour will be sold for a shekel, and two measures of barley for a shekel, in the gate of Samaria."

5. Court
    a. **Deuteronomy 16:18** - "You shall appoint for yourself judges and officers in all your towns which the LORD your God is giving you, according to your tribes, and they shall judge the people with righteous judgment.
    b. **Proverbs 8:1-3** - Does not wisdom call, And understanding lift up her voice? On top of the heights beside the way, Where the paths meet, she takes her stand; Beside the gates, at the opening to the city, At the entrance of the doors, she cries out:

6. Royal Castle/Palace
    a. **Deuteronomy 6:8-9** - "You shall bind them as a sign on your hand and they shall be as frontals on your forehead. 9"You shall write them on the doorposts of your house and on your gates. 10"Then it shall come about when the LORD your God brings you into the land which He swore to your fathers, Abraham, Isaac and Jacob, to give you, great and splendid cities which you did not build…"

7. Temple/Court
    a. **Jeremiah 7:2 -** "Stand in the gate of the LORD'S house and proclaim there this word and say, 'Hear the word of the LORD, all you of Judah, who enter by these gates to worship the LORD!'"
    b. **Psalm 118:19** – "Open to me the gates of righteousness; I shall enter through them, I shall give thanks to the LORD."
    c. **Esther 5:13** – "Yet all of this does not satisfy me every time I see Mordecai, the Jew, sitting at the king's gate.

8. Heaven
    a. **Genesis 28:10-17** - "10 Then Jacob departed from Beersheba and went toward Haran. 11 He came to a certain place and spent the night there, because the sun had set; and he took one of the <u>stones of the place</u> and put it under his head, and lay down in that place. 12 He had a dream, and behold, a ladder was set on the earth with its top **reaching** to heaven; and behold, the angels of God were ascending and descending on it. 13 And behold, the Lord stood above it and said, "I am the Lord, the God of your father Abraham and the God of Isaac; the land on which you lie, I will give it to you and to your descendants.

14 Your descendants will also be like the dust of the earth, and you will spread out to the west and to the east and to the north and to the south; and in you and in your descendants shall all the families of the earth be blessed. Behold, I am with you and will keep you wherever you go, and will bring you back to this land; for I will not leave you until I have done what I have promised you." 16 Then Jacob awoke from his sleep and said, "Surely the Lord is in this place, and I did not know it." 17 He was afraid and said, "How awesome is this place! This is none other than the house of God, and this is the **gate of heaven**."

- - - i. *Ezekiel 36:26* - "Moreover, I will give you a new heart and put a new spirit within you; and I will remove the heart of stone from your flesh and give you a heart of flesh."
  - b. **Revelation 4:1** - After these things I looked, and behold, a door standing open in heaven, and the first voice which I had heard, like the sound of a trumpet speaking with me, said, *"Come up here, and I will show you what must take place after these things."*
  - c. **Notice** the top of the ladder (stairway) didn't extend into heaven, but rather to heaven.
    - i. **Vs 13** states the Lord stood above it and said, "I am the Lord, the God of your father Abraham and the God of Isaac; the land on which you lie, I will give it to you and to your descendants.
      1. **Ephesians 2:6** - And raised us up with Him, and seated us with Him in the heavenly places in Christ Jesus…
      2. **Revelation 21:21** - And the twelve gates were twelve pearls; each one of the gates was a single pearl. And the street of the city was pure gold, like transparent glass.

9. Sheol
    a. **Job 38:17** - "Have the gates of death been revealed to you, Or have you seen the gates of deep darkness?
    b. **Matthew 16:18-19** – 'I also say to you that you are Peter, and upon this [d]rock I will build My church; and the gates of Hades will not overpower it. 19 I will give you the keys of the kingdom of heaven; and whatever you bind on earth shall have been bound in heaven, and whatever you loose on earth shall have been loosed in heaven."

III. WHAT OCCURRED AT THE GATES?

- GATE OF WORSHIP
  - **Psalm 100:4** - Enter His gates with thanksgiving, and His courts with praise. Give thanks to Him, bless His name.
  - **Psalm 122:1-2** – "I was glad when they said to me, "Let us go to the house of the LORD." Our feet are standing within your gates, O Jerusalem."
  - **Psalm 141:3** – "Set a guard, O Lord, over my mouth; Keep watch over the door of my lips [to keep me from speaking thoughtlessly]."
    - **Proverbs 18:21** – "Death and life are in the power of the tongue, and those who love it will eat its fruit."
    - **Proverbs 24:7** – "Wisdom is too high for a fool, He does not open his mouth in the gate."

- GATE OF JUDGEMENT
  - **Exodus 32:26** – "Then Moses stood in the **gate of the camp**, and said, "Whoever is for the Lord, come to me!" And all the sons of Levi gathered together to him."

- GATE OF DELIVERANCE & HEALING
  - **Isaiah 45:2** – (NKJV) "I will go before you and make the crooked places straight; I will break in pieces the gates of bronze (brass) and cut the bars of iron."
  - **Psalm 127:5** (NLT) – "How joyful is the man whose quiver is full of them! He will not be put to shame when he confronts his *accusers* at the city gates."
    - **Revelation 12:10** – "Then I heard a loud voice in heaven, saying, "Now the salvation, and the power, and the kingdom of our God and the **authority of His Christ** have come, for the accuser of our brethren has been thrown down, he who accuses them before our God day and night."
    - **2 Corinthians 2:11** – "So that no advantage would be taken of us by Satan, for we are not ignorant of his schemes."

- o **Acts 3:1-2, 6** (Amp) – "Now Peter and John were going up to the temple at the hour of prayer, the ninth hour (3:00 p.m.), 2 and a man who had been unable to walk from birth was being carried along, whom they used to set down every day at that gate of the temple which is called [a]Beautiful... 6 But Peter said, "Silver and gold I do not have; but what I do have I give to you: In the name (authority, power) of Jesus Christ the Nazarene—[begin now to] walk and go on walking!"

- GATE OF PROCLAMATIONS & DECLARATIONS
  - o **Proverbs 1:21** - At the head of the noisy streets she cries out; At the entrance of the gates in the city she utters her sayings:
  - o **Jeremiah 17:19** - Thus the LORD said to me, "Go and stand in the public gate, through which the kings of Judah come in and go out, as well as in all the gates of Jerusalem;

- GATE OF LEGAL AGREEMENTS
  - o *Contractual agreements-* **Genesis 23:7-10**
    - "So Abraham rose and bowed to the people of the land, the sons of Heth. 8 And he spoke with them, saying, "If it is your [e]wish for me to bury my dead out of my sight, hear me, and approach Ephron the son of Zohar for me, 9 that he may give me the cave of Machpelah which he owns... 10 [b]and Ephron the Hittite answered Abraham in the hearing of the sons of Heth; even of all who went in at the gate of his city, saying"
  - o *MARRIAGE AGREEMENTS* – **Ruth 4:10-11** (Amp)
    - Then Boaz went up to the city gate [where business and legal matters were settled] and sat down, and then the close relative (redeemer) of whom Boaz had spoken came by... 11 All the people at the gate and the elders said, "We are witnesses. May the Lord make the woman who is coming into your house like Rachel and Leah, the two who built the household of Israel. May you achieve wealth and power in Ephrathah and become famous in Bethlehem.
- GATE OF RIVER
  - o **Nahum 2:6** - The gates of the rivers are opened, and the palace is dissolved

- GATE OF ADMINISTRATION OF JUSTICE/JUDICIAL SYSTEM/REFUGEE
    - **Deut. 21:19** (NLT) - In such a case, the father and mother must take the son to the elders as they hold court at the town gate.
    - **Amos 5:10** (Amp) - They hate the one who reprimands [the unrighteous] in the [court held at the city] gate [regarding him as unreasonable and rejecting his reprimand], And they detest him who speaks [the truth] with integrity and honesty.
    - **Joshua 20:4** - He shall flee to one of these cities, and shall stand at the entrance of the gate of the city and state his case in the hearing of the elders of that city; and they shall take him into the city to them and give him a place, so that he may dwell among them.
    - **Proverbs 22:22** - Do not rob the poor because he is poor, or crush the afflicted at the gate;

- GATE OF PROMINENCE
    - **Proverbs 31:23** (NLT) - Her husband is well known at the city gates, where he sits with the other civic leaders.

- GATE OF BLESSING
    - **Zechariah 8:15-16** (NLT) – "So I have again purposed in these days to do good to Jerusalem and to the house of Judah. Do not fear! These are the things which you should do: <u>speak the truth to one another</u>; judge with truth and judgment for peace in your gates.

- GATE OF WAR
    - **Judges 5:7-8** - "The peasantry ceased, they ceased in Israel, Until I, Deborah, arose, Until I arose, a mother in Israel. 8"New gods were chosen; Then war was in the gates. Not a shield or a spear was seen Among forty thousand in Israel. 9"My heart goes out to the commanders of Israel, The volunteers among the people; Bless the LORD!...
    - **Hosea 11:6** (Amp) - The sword will whirl against and fall on their cities, and will demolish the bars of their gates and fortifications and will consume them because of their counsels.
    - **Judges 9:52-53** – "So Abimelech came to the tower and fought against it, and approached the entrance of the tower to burn it with fire. 53 But a certain woman threw an upper millstone on Abimelech's head, crushing his skull."

SESSION TWO

The gatekeepers were on the four sides, to the east, west, north and south.
(I Chronicles 9:24)

I. GATEKEEPERS

Gatekeepers where a vital part of societal life in the wilderness and during the reign of both King David and his successor King Solomon. Gatekeepers were essentially guards positioned at the various gates for protection, this included the gate of the tabernacle and temple. The [Levitical Priesthood], was charged with guarding the Lord's house.

Cities of old, had high, thick walls around them to keep out invading armies. Some of the gates where gatekeepers were positioned, are the city gates, palace gates, and the temple gates. Whoever controls the gates rules the [city, region, & nation]!

A gatekeeper is:

- One who tends or guards a gate
- A person who controls access
- Trustworthy
- Sober-minded *(clear judgement)*
- Vigilant/alert for any sign of trouble

    - **I Chronicles 9:22** - All these who were chosen to be gatekeepers at the thresholds were 212. These were enrolled by genealogy in their villages, whom David and Samuel the seer appointed in their office of trust.
    - **II Samuel 18:28** - "Then the *watchman* saw another man running, and he called down to the **gatekeeper**, 'Look, another man running alone!"
    - **I Peter 5:8** - Be of sober spirit, be on the alert. Your adversary, the devil, prowls around like a roaring lion, seeking someone to devour.

As previously stated, biblical cities had high walls, thick gates and deep trenches around them to keep invading armies out *(2 Chronicles 14:7)*. If the invading army/enemy conquered the gate, then they would control the [city, region, territory]. In both war and peace time, gates where significant. The [gatekeepers, watchmen, & elders] where positioned at the gate to observe the entrance and exit of everyone to ensure to safety of its inhabitants. To conquer a city and occupy its territory, gates where attacked by smashing them with battering rams and fire.

- **Ezekiel 26:9** - "The blow of his battering rams he will direct against your walls, and with his axes he will break down your towers.
- **II Chronicles 36:19** – "Then they burned the house of God and broke down the wall of Jerusalem, and burned all its fortified buildings with fire and destroyed all its valuable articles."
  - **Jeremiah 21:10** - "For I have set My face against this city for harm and not for good," declares the LORD. "It will be given into the hand of the king of Babylon and he will burn it with fire."'
- **Amos 1:14** - "So I will kindle a fire on the wall of Rabbah and it will consume her citadels amid war cries on the day of battle, and a storm on the day of tempest."

Gates, gatekeepers, walls and watchmen can also symbolize a **defensive** position *(protection from any impending danger)* or an **offensive** position *(storming the gates or walls of the enemy)*. Remember the gates of Babylon (defensive); were thought to be impregnable, but when God sets HIS face against a {region, city, territory}; nothing can stop its destruction.

- **Isaiah 45:1-2** – "Thus says the LORD to Cyrus His anointed, Whom I have taken by the right hand, To subdue nations before him and to loose the loins of kings; To open doors before him so that gates will not be shut: "I will go before you and make the rough places smooth; I will shatter the doors of bronze and cut through their iron bars...."

Gatekeepers secure the entrance of churches, cities, regions, families, schools, business, etc., and make sure [doors/gates] are opened and closes accordingly. They are sensitive to the level of activities that occur at the entrance and stand guard to ensure nothing unwanted enters. Gatekeepers are armed and have powerful pray authority, working with Holy Spirit to ensure that the atmosphere is conducive. Gatekeepers are saturated in God's Presence individually and release corporately to the body of Christ.

- **John 10:2-3** *(Amp)* – "But he who enters by the door is the shepherd of the sheep [the protector and provider]. 3 The [a]doorkeeper opens [the gate] for this man, and the sheep hear his voice and pay attention to it. And [knowing that they listen] he calls his own sheep by name and leads them out [to pasture]."
- **Matthew 16:19** - "I will give you the keys of the kingdom of heaven; and whatever you bind on earth shall have been bound in heaven, and whatever you loose on earth shall have been loosed in heaven."
- **Revelation 3:7** - "And to the angel of the church in Philadelphia write: He who is holy, who is true, who has the key of David, who opens and no one will shut, and who shuts and no one opens, says this:"

A gatekeeper that is slack in his/her duties could bring destruction upon an entire region. So at the core, gatekeepers/doorkeepers must be alert and on guard to protect. When gatekeepers and watchmen are not trustworthy, of sober mind, vigilant, and discerning of spirits the inhabitants are in danger of (1) oppression, & (2) injustice.

- **Lamentations 4:12** - The kings of the earth did not believe, nor did any of the inhabitants of the world, that the adversary and the enemy could enter the gates of Jerusalem.
- **Ezekiel 22:29-30** - The people of the land have practiced oppression and committed robbery, and they have <u>wronged the poor and needy</u> and have <u>oppressed the sojourner</u> without justice. 30 I searched for a man among them who would **build up the wall** and *stand in the gap* before Me for the land, so that I would not destroy it; but I found no one.

II. GATEKEEPERS IN THE WILDERNESS

As the children of Israel journeyed through the wilderness of Sinai, gatekeepers were appointed by the Lord to guard the Holy Place and the nation of Israel. Before they were able to possess the promised land, God instructed Moses to number the warriors, the gatekeepers that guard the entire nation of Israel. Chief gatekeepers were selected from among the twelve tribes, each one a head of his father's household *(Numbers 1:4)*. The number of warriors counted in the wilderness totaled 603,550.

The Levites were exempt from being numbered because they were appointed over the tabernacle of the testimony, and over all its furnishings and over all that belongs to it *(Numbers 1:50)*. They were the gatekeepers of the Lord's house and would therefore camp around the tabernacle of testimony, so the wrath of God would not come upon the congregation of the sons of Israel. The Lord further commanded Moses to arrange the sons of Israel by his own standard, with the banners of their father's households; they shall encamp at a distance. *(Numbers 2:2)*

EAST GATE	EAST GATE
o Judah- **praise** o Issachar-**recompense** o Zebulun-**dwelling**	o Aaronites ▪ Descendants of Aaron and Moses
SOUTH GATE	**SOUTH GATE**
o Reuben-**behold thy son** o Simeon-**God hears** o Gad-**good fortune**	o Kohathites: ▪ Descendants of Kohath, *second son of Levi*, Aaron and Moses were Kohathites but had a different authority
WEST GATE	**WEST GATE**
o Ephraim-**double fruitfulness** o Manasseh-**made to forget** o Benjamin-**son of my right hand**	o Gershonites: ▪ Descendants of Gershon/Gershon, *first son of Levi*
NORTH GATE	**NORTH GATE**
o Dan-**judge** o Asher-**happy/laughter** o Naphtali-**my wrestling**	o Merarites: ▪ Descendants of Merari, *third son of Levi*

The LORD spoke to Moses, saying, "Make yourself two trumpets of silver, of hammered work you shall make them; and you shall use them for summoning the congregation and for having the camps set out **(Numbers 10:1-2)**. The trumpets were two in number, symbolic of their <u>devotion</u> to <u>witnessing</u>. The two silver trumpets could only be blown by the priest **(Numbers 10:8)**, and the word declares that we are PRIEST..."But you are a chosen race, A royal priesthood, a holy nation, a people for god's own possession, so that you may proclaim the excellency of Him who has called you out of darkness into His marvelous light **(I Peter 2:9)**.

In **I Corinthians 14:8**, the Apostle Paul writes, "If the trumpets give an uncertain voice, who shall prepare himself for war?" So as a gatekeepers of the Lord's house, our sound must be clear and precise so that the people will assemble in battle array prepared for war.

> 13 So they moved out for the first time according to the commandment of the Lord through Moses. 14 The standard of the camp of the sons of Judah, according to their armies, set out first,... 17 Then the tabernacle was taken down; and the sons of Gershon and the sons of Merari, who were carrying the tabernacle, set out. 18 Next the standard of the camp of Reuben, according to their armies, set out with Elizur the son of Shedeur, over its army... *(Numbers 10:13-18)*

The Tabernacle began at Mt. Sinai in 1446 BC and it was at that time that duties were given to each of the three lines of priests, but only the sons of Aaron could offer animal sacrifices or incense. Levites were assigned and located in every city, not just the 48 Levitical cities (Deuteronomy 18:6-7). The priesthood continued down to the destruction of Jerusalem in 70 AD when it became naturally extinct, but it became spiritually extinct at the death of Christ; who is our High Priest & King forever!

III. DAVIDIC ORDER OF GATEKEEPERS

According to (**1 Chronicles 9:22**), King David and Samuel the Seer appointed 212 gatekeepers for "positions of trust" in guarding the temple of the Lord and their relatives who were appointed to rotate for 7 day assignments *(verse 25)*. The gatekeepers spent the night positioned around the house of God, as they did in the wilderness, and they also had charge of the **gate key** for *opening* and *closing* the **gate** each morning and night respectively. Temple gatekeepers/doorkeepers were in charge of who went in and out to ensure order and reverence for God's house.

> 17 Now the gatekeepers were Shallum and Akkub and Talmon and Ahiman and their relatives (Shallum the chief 18 being stationed until now at the king's gate to the east). These were the gatekeepers for the camp of the sons of Levi. 19 Shallum the son of Kore, the son of Ebiasaph, the son of Korah, and his relatives of his father's house, the Korahites, were over the work of the service, keepers of the thresholds of the tent; and their fathers had been over the camp of the Lord, keepers of the entrance. 20 Phinehas the son of Eleazar was ruler over them previously, and the Lord was with him. 21 Zechariah the son of Meshelemiah was gatekeeper of the entrance of the tent of meeting. 22 All these who were chosen to be gatekeepers at the thresholds were 212. These were enrolled by genealogy in their villages, whom **David and Samuel** the seer *appointed* in their office of trust. *(I Chronicles 9:17-22)*

The gatekeepers and watchmen were not the same person as identified in (**2 Samuel 18:26**). Watchmen were the Prophets that had strong discernment and kept {watch} over the city. In today's spiritual climate, this can be seen as an apostolic/prophetic gift. The gatekeepers were the guards stationed at the entrance of the [city, region, nation], and who work in conjunction with the Apostolic/Prophetic voice (watchmen), to control entrance and exits and secure the territory.

- **Isaiah 62:6** - On your walls, O Jerusalem, I have appointed watchmen; All day and all night they will never keep silent. You who remind the LORD, take no rest for yourselves;
- **Ezekiel 33:6** - 'But if the watchman sees the sword coming and does not blow the trumpet and the people are not warned, and a sword comes and takes a person from them, he is taken away in his iniquity; but his blood I will require from the watchman's hand.'

IV. DUTIES OF GATEKEEPERS

The gatekeepers are stationed at the four corners of the sanctuary: east, west, north & south – to prevent invasions from every direction (v. 24), with the chief of the gatekeepers, Shallum, stationed at the east gate, in the place previously reserved for priests (vv. 17-18). Being a gatekeeper/doorkeeper requires you to set the standard *or* bear the standard that has been established by the Lord.

> **I Chronicles 26:12** - To these divisions of the gatekeepers, the chief men, were given duties like their relatives to minister in the house of the Lord.

- **Spiritual guards:** Gatekeepers/doorkeepers over [families, churches, cities, businesses and nations] to monitor those that enter and exit along with controlling the spiritual climate.
    - **Matthew 12:43-45**
    - **John 10:1-9**
- **Warfare Strategist:** The gates of ancient cities were the place of decision making. These gates were the place the elders of the city met to consider important matters.
    - **Exodus 18:16** – "When they have a dispute, it comes to me [at the tent of meetings], and I judge between a man and his neighbor and make known the statutes of God and His laws."
    - **Job 29:7** – "When I went out to the gate of the city, when I took my seat [as a city father] in the square,"
- **Guards {Priesthood & Kingdom Keys}:** Gatekeepers open and close the doors of God's Temple and <u>hold the keys</u> to the Lord's house. They were chosen from the Levitical priesthood and set in place by the prophetic office, of Samuel the Seer; under the authority of King David.
    - **I Chronicles 9:27** – "They spent the night around the house of God, because the watch was committed to them; and they were in charge of opening it morning by morning."
    - **I Chronicles 9:23** – "So they and their sons had charge of the gates of the house of the Lord, even the house of the tent, as guards."

Matthew 16:19 (Amp) –" I will give you the keys (authority) of the kingdom of heaven; and whatever you bind [forbid, declare to be improper and unlawful]

King David ordered "the Levites to be numbered from thirty years old and upward, and their number by census of men was 38,000. Of these, 24,000 were to oversee the work of the house of the Lord; and 6,000 were officers and judges, and **4,000 were gatekeepers,** and <u>4,000 were praising the Lord</u> with the instruments which David made for giving praise. David divided them into divisions according to the sons of Levi: Gershon, Kohath, and Merari"

(I Chronicles 23:3-6)

- The Levites being numbered was based on the biblical command found in Numbers 4:1-3, indicating that a Levite's service began at 30 years of age.

- The 38,000 qualified Levites were divided into divisions and given duties:
    - **Oversee the work of the house of the Lord:** There was a lot of activity that transpired at the temple {worship, sacrifices, festivals, etc}.
    - **Officers and judges:** As civil servants for the nation of Israel, the Levites handled all governmental matters, contracts, records and administration.
    - **Gatekeepers:** They were responsible for the safety of Israel, both in natural and spiritual matters.
    - **4,000 praised the Lord:** They were responsible for worshipping God both with their voices and musical instruments.
    - **David separated them into divisions among the sons of Levi:** *Gershon, Kohath, and Merari:*
        - **Gershon:** The Gershonites were to take care of the skins that covered the tabernacle itself.
        - **Kohath:** The Kohathites were to take care of the furniture of the tabernacle including the ark of the covenant, the table of showbread, and so forth, under the direction of Eleazar the priest, son of Aaron.
        - **Merari:** The Merarites were responsible for taking care of the structural aspects of the tabernacle including the pillars, the boards, and so forth

V. ASSIGNMENT OF GATES

The lot to the <u>east</u> fell to **Shelemiah**. Then they cast lots for his son **Zechariah**, a counselor with insight, and his lot came out to the <u>north</u>. 15 For **Obed-edom** it fell to the <u>south</u>, and to his sons went the storehouse. 16 For **Shuppim and Hosah** it was to the <u>west</u>, by the gate of Shallecheth, on the ascending highway. Guard corresponded to guard. 17 On the east there were six Levites, on the north four daily, on the south four daily, and at the storehouse two by two. At the Parbar on the west there were four at the highway and two at the Parbar.

I Chronicles 26:14-18

- **EAST GATE**
  - *Shelemiah-means (1) friend of God, (2) He will restore or repay*
    - **Ezekiel 44:1-2** - Then He brought me back by the way of the outer gate of the sanctuary, which faces the east; and it was shut. 2 The Lord said to me, "This gate shall be shut; it shall not be opened, and no one shall enter by it, for the Lord God of Israel has entered by it; therefore it shall be shut…"
      - **Ezekiel 11:1-4** - Then the Spirit lifted me and took me to the east gate of the Lord's temple. (It's the gate that faces east.) Twenty-five men were at the entrance of the gate…They were leaders of the people. Then the Lord said to me, "Son of man, these are the men who plan evil and give bad advice in this city. 3 They say, 'It's almost time to rebuild homes. This city is a cooking pot, and we're the meat.' 4So prophesy against them. Prophesy, son of man."

- **NORTH GATE**
  - *Zechariah-means the Lord is REMEMBERED*
    - **Ezekiel 44:4** - Then He brought me by way of the north gate to the front of the house; and I looked, and behold, the glory of the LORD filled the house of the LORD, and I fell on my face..
      - **Ezekiel 8:3** – "He stretched out the form of a hand and took me by a lock of hair on my head; and the Spirit lifted me up between earth and heaven and brought me in the visions of God to Jerusalem, to the entrance of the north gate of the inner courtyard, where the seat of the idol of jealousy, which provokes to jealousy, was located."

- **WEST GATE**
  - *Shuppim & Hosah-means [serpent **or** storehouse & refuge, respectively]*
    -

- **SOUTH GATE**
  - *Obed-Edom-means (1) worshipper & (2) servant*
    - **Ezekiel 40:44** - From the outside to the inner gate were chambers for the singers in the inner court, one of which was at the side of the north gate, with its front toward the south, and one at the side of the south gate facing toward the north.

Ezekiel 48:30-35 - "These are the exits of the city: on the **north side**, 4,500 *cubits* by measurement, ³¹shall be the gates of the city, named for the tribes of Israel, three gates toward the north: the gate of **Reuben**, one; the gate of **Judah**, one; the gate of **Levi**, one. ³² On the **east side**, 4,500 *cubits*, shall be three gates: the gate of **Joseph**, one; the gate of **Benjamin**, one; the gate of **Dan**, one. ³³ On the **south side**, 4,500 *cubits* by measurement, shall be three gates: the gate of **Simeon**, one; the gate of **Issachar**, one; the gate of **Zebulun**, one.³⁴ On the **west side**, 4,500 *cubits*, *shall be* three gates: the gate of Gad, one; the gate of Asher, one; the gate of Naphtali, one. ³⁵ *The city shall be* 18,000 *cubits* round about; and the name of the city from *that* day *shall be*, 'The LORD is there.'

Wilderness	*Post-Wilderness*
o EAST GATE ▪ Judah, Issachar & Zebulun	o **North Gate** ▪ **Reuben, Judah & Levi**
o South Gate ▪ Reuben, Simeon & Gad	o East Gate ▪ Joseph, Benjamin & Dan
o West Gate ▪ Ephraim, Manasseh &, Benjamin	o South Gate ▪ Simeon, Issachar & Zebulun
o NORTH GATE ▪ Dan, Asher & Naphtali	o West Gate ▪ Gad, Asher and Naphtali

Aren't you glad that you don't look like what you've been through? The strategies and tactics that you executed in the wilderness are not the same tools that are required in the promised land. Ezekiel prophecy provides insight for John's vision found in the book of Revelation:

- **Revelation 21:10-12** - 10 And he carried me away in the Spirit to a great and high mountain, and showed me the holy city, Jerusalem, coming down out of heaven from God, 11 having the glory of God. Her brilliance was like a very costly stone, as a stone of crystal-clear jasper. 12 It had a great and high wall, with twelve gates, and at the **gates twelve angels**; and names were written on them, which are the names of *the twelve tribes of the sons of Israel.*"

Here we see 12 gates, being guarded by 12 Angels, representing "governmental authority"; both naturally and spiritually. They are positioned strategically at the (East, South, North & West Gates, respectively), and the names written on each of the Angels, was that of "sons of Israel." We previously learned that hades has gates, which we could deduce that hades also has guards stationed at the gates as well.

Nancy Kaplan, author of Weapons of Mass Deliverance, has a list of 12 strongholds that contend with the 12 gates, based on a teaching by Pastor Benny Hinn. For a more in-depth look, please search for her book online.

12 Gates/12 Angels	12 Strongholds
Reuben – Behold the son	Anti-Christ
Simeon – Hearing	Deaf & Dumb Spirit
Judah – Let God be praised	Perversion
Zebulon – Dwelling place	Familiar Spirits
Asher – Happy/Laughter	Spirit of Heaviness
Gad – Good fortune	Spirit of Fear
Naphtali – wrestling	Spirit of Jealousy
Dan – Judge	Spirit of Bondage
Issachar – Man of Hire	Spirit of Whoredom
Benjamin – Son of my right hand	Spirit of Pride
Joseph – One who increases	Spirit of Infirmity
Levi – Joined to God	Lying Spirit

We know that the enemy wants to control the gates, in order to control the region. We see an account of the enemy at the gate in the book of Ezekiel.

- **Ezekiel 8:5** "Then He said to me, "Son of man, raise your eyes now toward the north." So I raised my eyes toward the north, and behold, to the north of the altar gate was this idol of jealousy at the entrance."

Therefore, we must ensure that those assigned to the gates take their position and displace the enemy at the gate along with the Angelic Host that labor among us. Remember we can only say what we have heard our Father say. And **Psalm 127:5** reminds us that "we will not be ashamed, when we speak with the enemy in the gates."

- **Jeremiah 1:12** -Then the Lord said to me, "You have seen well, for I am watching over My word to perform it."
- **Psalm 103:20** - Bless the Lord, you His angels, mighty in strength, who perform His word, obeying the voice of His word!
- **Psalm 34:7** - The angel of the Lord encamps around those who fear Him, and rescues them.
- **Genesis 3:24** - So He drove the man out; and at the east of the garden of Eden He stationed the cherubim and the flaming sword which turned every direction to guard the way to the tree of life.

As we can see, Angels have be gatekeepers/guards, protecting the word of God. They have also be charged with the task of guarding us…

- **Psalm 91:11** – "For He will give His angels charge concerning you, To guard you in all your ways."
- **2 Kings 6:17** Then Elisha prayed and said, "O Lord, I pray, open his eyes that he may see." And the Lord opened the servant's eyes and he saw; and behold, the mountain was full of horses and chariots of fire all around Elisha.

SESSION THREE

"indeed I will greatly bless you, and I will greatly multiply your seed as the stars of the heavens and as the sand which is on the seashore; and your seed shall possess the gate of their enemies." **Genesis 22:17**

I. POSSESSING THE GATES

The Hebrew words for **possess** is <u>yarash</u> and it means *[to seize, to dispossess, take possession off, inherit, disinherit, **occupy**, impoverish, to destroy, bring to ruin, spiritual power and authority]*. Gates speak of rules and a place of counsel. The book of Proverbs is filled with analogies referring to gates as a place where people received counsel/wisdom from the elders at the gates. The elders and/or dignitaries at the gates were perceived to be people who had (1) wisdom, (2) knew counsel, and (3) understood laws and regulations. Remember our battle is not against "flesh & blood", **(Eph. 6:12)**. God's plan for your life will be established and the strategy of the enemy will not prosper.

> "No weapon that is formed against you will succeed; And every tongue that rises against you in judgment you will condemn. This [peace, righteousness, security, and triumph over opposition] is the heritage of the servants of the Lord, And this is their vindication from Me," says the Lord ***(Isaiah 54:17)***

The tactics of the enemy have not changed and his ultimate goal against the church is to [kills, steal and destroy] – **John 10:10**. As we prepare for war, declare that the Lord of Host will give us strength for the battle:

> "A spirit of justice for him who sits in judgment [administering the law], A strength to those who drive back the battle at the gate." ***(Isaiah 28:6-Amp)***

In our cities, states, nations today, it appears as though the enemy of the Kingdom of God has possessed our "gates." The enemy is indicative of ideologies and principals that oppose Word of God. One of the tactics of the enemy is his use propaganda to:

> 19 Then Rabshakeh said to them, "Say now to Hezekiah, 'Thus says the great king, the king of Assyria, "What is this confidence that you have? *(2 Kings 18:19)*

The enemy uses *"propaganda"* to incite fear:
- influences business climate
- control the culture of a nation
- sabotage relationships in social circles
- derail the political infrastructure, &
- destroy the church.

Possessing the Gates are symbolic of taking the strength, power, and dominion of a nation.
- **Psalm 24:7** – "Lift up your heads, O gates, And be lifted up, O ancient doors, That the King of glory may come in!"
- **Isaiah 45:1-2 (TLB)** – "This is Jehovah's message to Cyrus, God's anointed, whom he has chosen to conquer many lands. God shall empower his right hand, and he shall crush the strength of mighty kings. God shall open the gates of Babylon to him; the gates shall not be shut against him anymore. 2 I will go before you, Cyrus, and level the mountains and smash down the city gates of brass and iron bars."

Possessing the gates, allows us to (1) enter the door, or (2) exit the gate into something greater. By taking authority over the gates, we can shut the enemy down and close any potential doors that he may be using gain access in our region. God wants to heal our land. He longs to restore generational blessings that have been held back or tied up in your generational line.

- "then if my people will humble themselves and pray, and search for me, and turn from their wicked ways, I will hear them from heaven and forgive their sins and heal their land." *(II Chronicles 7:14 - TLB)*

Watchtowers were constructed above the corners of the gates so that the watchmen could see when an enemy was approaching and call to the gatekeeper, who would alert the city.

- **II Chronicles 14:7** – "For he said to Judah, "Let us build these cities and surround them with <u>walls and towers</u>, **gates and bars.** The land is still ours because we have sought the Lord our God; we have sought Him, and He has given us rest on every side." So they built and prospered."
- **II Samuel 18:25-26** – The watchman called and told the king. And the king said, "If he is by himself there is good news in his mouth." And he came nearer and nearer. 26 Then the watchman saw another man running; and the watchman called to the gatekeeper and said, "Behold, another man running by himself." And the king said, "This one also is bringing good news."

At night, the gates were closed, **secured** by <u>locks with keys</u>, and guarded by gatekeepers.

- **Joshua 2:7** So the [king's] men pursued them on the road to the Jordan as far as the [b]fords [east of Jericho]; as soon as the pursuers had gone out after them, the gate [of the city] was shut.
- **Nehemiah 7:3** - Then I said to them, "Do not let the gates of Jerusalem be opened until the sun is hot, and while they are standing guard, let them shut and bolt the doors. Also appoint guards from the inhabitants of Jerusalem, each at his post, and each in front of his own house."

There were several ways to gain access to a region, some of which include the use of a (1) battering ram, with (2) fire or a (3) key:

- **Ezekiel 26:9** - "The blow of his battering rams he will direct against your walls, and with his axes he will break down your towers.
- **II Chronicles 36:19** - Then they burned the house of God and broke down the wall of Jerusalem, and burned all its fortified buildings with fire and destroyed all its valuable articles.
- **Matthew 16:19** - "I will give you the keys of the kingdom of heaven; and whatever you bind on earth shall have been bound in heaven, and whatever you loose on earth shall have been loosed in heaven."
    - **Isaiah 22:20-22** - And then I will call my servant Eliakim, the son of Hilkiah, to replace you. He shall have your uniform and title and authority, and he will be a father to the people of Jerusalem and all Judah.I will give him responsibility over all my people; whatever he says will be done; none will be able to stop him.

II. ACCESS GRANTED

> 19 I will give you the **keys (authority)** of the kingdom of heaven; and whatever you bind [forbid, declare to be improper and unlawful] on earth [a]will have [already] been bound in heaven, and whatever you loose [permit, declare lawful] on earth [b]will have [already] been loosed in heaven."
> *Matthew 16:19 - Amp*

The Greek word for **key** is *"kleis"*, which denotes power & authority; and it speaks of the keeper of the keys: the one who has the power to open and shut. The promise to possess the gate of our enemies refers to the possession of strategic points that **allow access** to or control over kingdoms/nations. In biblical accounts, a key was an symbol of governmental authority. Before we examine the significance of the key, let us first understand the Kingdom of Heaven. The bible tells us that the Kingdom is not a matter of our "presumable" free will, but instead:

> 17 for the Kingdom of God is not a matter of eating and drinking [what one likes], but of righteousness and peace and joy in the Holy Spirit. *(Romans 14:17)*

1. Righteousness
   - **Isaiah 26:2** - "Open the gates, that the righteous nation may enter, The one that remains faithful.
2. Peace
   - **Psalm 122:7** - "May peace be within your walls, And prosperity within your palaces."
3. Joy
   - **Psalm 100:4** - Enter His gates with thanksgiving And His courts with praise. Give thanks to Him, bless His name.

ENTERING THE KINGDOM:
- "Verily, verily, I say unto thee, Except a man be born again, he cannot see the Kingdom of God." **(John 3:3)**
- "Now I say this, brethren, that flesh and blood cannot inherit the kingdom of God; nor does [a]the perishable inherit [b]the imperishable." **(I Cor. 15:50)**
- "For God so loved the world, that He gave His [a]only begotten Son, that whoever believes in Him shall not perish, but have eternal life. For God did not send the Son into the world to judge the world, but that the world might be saved through Him

With this understanding of the Kingdom of Heaven, let us examine keys. The function of a key is to grant access to the keeper of the keys:

- **Authority**- Is used predominantly in the New Testament, where the word <u>exousia</u> functions in at least four ways.
    - Access
    - Power
    - Freedom
    - Sphere

I. The word **authority** makes reference to delegated authority, inclusive of the authorization to perform a task or assignment:
    - **Matthew 21:23** When He entered the temple, the chief priests and the elders of the people came to Him while He was teaching, and said, "By what authority are You doing these things, and who gave You this authority?"
    - **John 10:18** - "No one has taken it away from Me, but I lay it down on My own initiative. I have authority to lay it down, and I have authority to take it up again. This commandment I received from My Father."
    - **2 Corinthians 10:8** - So even if I boast somewhat freely about the authority the Lord gave us for building you up rather than tearing you down, I will not be ashamed of it.

II. Authority also refers to the **power**, to execute a command or to complete a task. Essentially, authority is useless without the power enforce:
    - **Matthew 9:6-8** "But so that you may know that the Son of Man has authority on earth to forgive sins "-then He said to the paralytic, "Get up, pick up your bed and go home." 7 And he got up and went home. 8 But when the crowds saw this, they were awestruck, and glorified God, who had given such authority to men.
    - **Mark 6:7** - And He summoned the twelve and began to send them out in pairs, and gave them authority over the unclean spirits;
    - **Luke 10:19** - "Behold, I have given you authority to tread on serpents and scorpions, and over all the power of the enemy, and nothing will injure you.

III. Authority begins and ends with God and thus our **freedom** is in God:
   - **Romans 13:1** Every person is to be in subjection to the governing authorities, For there is no authority except from God, and those which exist are established by God.
   - **Romans 9:21** Or does not the potter have a right over the clay, to make from the same lump one vessel for honorable use and another * for common use?
   - **Acts 1:7** - He said to them, "It is not for you to know times or epochs which the Father has fixed by His own authority;
   - **1 Co 9:18** - What then is my reward? That, when I preach the gospel, I may offer the gospel without charge, so as not to make full use of my right in the gospel..
   - **1 Co 8:9** - But take care that this liberty of yours does not somehow become a stumbling block to the weak.

IV. God has established spheres of authority, which are indicative of the space where we execute our God given authority.
   - **Luke 23:7** – "And when he learned that He belonged to Herod's jurisdiction, he sent Him to Herod, who himself also was in Jerusalem at that time."
   - **Ephesians 1:20-21** - "which He brought about in Christ, when He raised Him from the dead and seated Him at His right hand in the heavenly places, 21 far above all rule and authority and power and dominion, and every name that is named, not only in this age but also in the one to come."
   - **Titus 3:1** Remind them to be subject to rulers, to authorities, to be obedient, to be ready for every good deed,
   - **Colossians 1:13** - For He rescued us from the domain of darkness, and transferred us to the kingdom of His beloved Son,

V. Ultimately, the Keys of the Kingdom <u>grant us access</u> to ALL Truth!
   - **John 16:13** - "But when He, the Spirit of truth, comes, He will guide you into all the truth; for He will not speak on His own initiative, but whatever He hears, He will speak; and He will disclose to you what is to come.

The religious leaders in Jesus' day had arrogantly **taken away** the key to knowledge, such that neither them, nor their hearers entered in.

- *Key to Knowledge:*
    - **Proverbs 1:7** – "The fear of the LORD is the beginning of knowledge; Fools despise wisdom and instruction."
        - **Luke 11:52** – "Woe to you lawyers, because you have taken away the key to knowledge (scriptural truth). You yourselves did not enter, and you held back those who were entering [by your flawed interpretation of God's word and your man-made tradition]."
- **Matthew 28:18-20** - Then Jesus came to them and said, "**All authority** in heaven and on earth has been given to Me. 19Therefore go and make disciples of all nations, baptizing them in the name of the Father, and of the Son, and of the Holy Spirit, 20and teaching them to obey all that I have commanded you. And surely I am with you always, to the very end of the age."…

BATTLE POSITIONS

The key to knowledge has been revealed to us through Jesus Christ and we must endeavor to do all that the Father has need of us to do in this hour. **Ephesians 1:21** tells us that we are seated "far above all rule and authority and power and dominion, and every name that is named, not only in this age but also in the one to come." So if Jesus Christ is seated at the right hand of the Father and WE are one, then this verse implies that we are also seated in the heavenly realm at the right hand of the Father.

Therefore, we have authority over:
- Rule
- Authority
- Power
- Dominion
    - For our struggle is not against flesh and blood, but against the rulers, against the powers, against the world forces of this darkness, against the spiritual forces of wickedness in the heavenly places (**Eph. 6:12**).

VI. OCCUPY UNTIL JESUS RETURNS

"And he called ten of his slaves, and gave them ten minas and said to them, 'Engage in business with this until I come back.' (**Luke 19:13**)

We were commissioned to "do business/occupy" until Jesus returns. And just as Jesus was anointed and called to do the work of the Father, so are we also called to be His representatives in the earth realm, doing greater works than my Father.

> You know of Jesus of Nazareth, how God anointed Him with the Holy Spirit and with power, [b]and how He went about doing good and healing all who were **oppressed** by the devil, for God was with Him. **(Acts 10:38)**

The commission was inclusive of go forth and (1) cast out demons, (2) heal the sick, (3) raise the dead, (4) cleanse the lepers and (5) preach the gospel. Preaching the Gospel of the Kingdom is demonstrative of the love and power of the Father toward His people! Signs and wonders should follow us because we believe! Think of the lives that can be impacted by the Power of God's word manifesting in their life! Think of the ministry of {Peter, Paul and Philip}…how many people believed because they saw the power of God operating through them, healing the sick, casting out demons and performing many miracles:

> 7 And as you go, preach, saying, 'The kingdom of heaven is at hand.'
> Heal the sick, raise the dead, cleanse the lepers, cast out demons.
> Freely you received, freely give. **Matthew 10:7-8**

Engaging in business of our Father, will require EACH of us to use our gifts such that people are edified and God glorified. **Romans 12:6-8** - Since we have gifts that differ according to the grace given to us, *each of us is to exercise them accordingly*: if prophecy, according to the proportion of his faith; if service, in his serving; or he who teaches, in his teaching; or he who exhorts, in his exhortation; he who gives, with liberality; he who leads, with diligence; he who shows mercy, with cheerfulness.

VII. NEW ORDER OF WORSHIP

When God provided King David with the "blue print" for the temple, he also instructed him on the pattern for worship in the Tabernacle of David. King David along with Samuel the Seer, appointed and anointed the {minstrels, psalmist, musicians and dancers} for the work of ministry. According to **I Chronicles 28:19** "All this," said David, "the LORD made me understand in writing by His hand upon me, all the details of this pattern." King David also reorganized the priesthood into 24 divisions. These 24 divisions remained active until the [death, burial & resurrection] of Christ.

I. **Prophetic Davidic Worship**
   - 1 Chronicles 25:1
   - Psalm 46:10
   - Psalm 50:7
   - Psalm 85:8

II. **Holy Spirit Inspired songs**
   - Psalm 33:3
   - Psalm 96:1
   - Psalm 149:1

III. **Corporate Worship**
   - Psalm 34:3
   - Psalm 57:5
   - Psalm 35:18
   - Psalm 26:2

IV. **Presence of the Most High**
   - 1 Kings 8:11
   - Chronicles 5:14
   - Psalm 50:2.-4

II Chronicles 29:25 informs us that King David instituted this order of worship in conjunction with <u>Gad the king's seer and Nathan the prophet</u>, by the commandment of the Lord. King David stationed the Levites in the house of the Lord with cymbals, harps and lyres, according to the command from the Lord through His prophets.

- The Levites were numbered from thirty years old and upward, and their number by census of men was 38,000. 4 Of these, **24,000** were to oversee the work of the house of the Lord; and **6,000** *were officers and judges*, 5 and <u>**4,000** were gatekeepers</u>, and **4,000 were praising the Lord** with the instruments which David made for giving praise. 6 David divided them into divisions according to the sons of Levi: Gershon, Kohath, and Merari *(I Chronicles 23:3)*

  - **24,000** Overseers looked after the work of the house of the Lord: The temple was constantly flowing with worshippers, sacrifices, and service unto God. It required numerous skilled workers to take care of all the practical matters behind temple daily activities. *(I Chronicles 24)*

  - **6,000** Officers and judges: The Levites were civil servants responsible for the accuracy of governmental records, legal decisions, and the administration of the Kingdom's affairs. *(I Chronicles 26:29-32)*

  - **4,000** Gatekeepers: These had the responsibility for securing both in the natural and spiritual realm. They ensured that only those who were ready to serve and worship God in "Spirit & Truth", could ENTER the temple and its associated buildings. *(I Chronicles 26:1-19)*

  - **4,000** Praised the Lord: The Levites had the responsibility of worshipping God continuously. *(I Chronicles 25)*

Minstrel's, and Prophetic [Psalmist & Dancers] are very strategic in the body of Christ. All throughout history, we see this group going ahead of the army of the Lord in battle. The blueprint that Kind David instituted under the guidance of the Lord, called for anointed and skilled Levites.

- **I Chronicles 15:22** – Chenaniah, chief of the Levites, was in charge of the singing; he gave instruction in singing because he was skillful.
- **I Chronicles 25:1, 7**- Moreover, David and the commanders of the army set apart for the service some of the sons of Asaph and of Heman and of Jeduthun, who were to prophesy with lyres, harps and cymbals;… Their number who were <u>trained</u> in singing to the Lord, with their relatives, all who were <u>skillful,</u> was **288.**

I. **Armies defeated when we incorporate Praise & Worship:**
   - **II Chronicles 20:21-22** - When he had consulted with the people, **<u>he appointed those who sang to the Lord</u>** and those who praised Him in holy attire, as they went out before the army and said, "Give thanks to the Lord, for His lovingkindness is everlasting." 22 When *they began singing* and praising, the Lord set ambushes against the sons of Ammon, Moab and Mount Seir, who had come against Judah; so they were [a]routed.
   - **II Kings 3:15** But now bring me a **<u>minstrel</u>**." And it came about, when the minstrel played, that the hand of the Lord came upon him.
   - **Joshua 6:4** - Also seven priests shall carry seven trumpets of rams' horns before the ark; then on the seventh day you shall march around the city seven times, and the priests shall blow the trumpets.
   - **Judges 7:20, 22** When the three companies blew the trumpets and broke the pitchers, they held the torches in their left hands and the trumpets in their right hands for blowing, and cried, "A sword for the Lord and for Gideon!"… 22 When they blew 300 trumpets, the Lord set the sword of one against another even throughout the whole army;

References

Eckhardt, John. The Shamar Prophet. (2006). The Crusaders Ministries.

Kaplan, Nancy. Weapons of Mass Deliverance (2004). Xulon Press.

Munroe, Myles. Understanding your place in God's Kingdom. (2011). Destiny Image Publishers, Inc.

Pierce, Chuck, Heidler Robert & Heidler, Linda. A Time To Advance (2011). Glory of Zion International. https://gloryofzion.org//webstore/Scripts/prodView.asp?idproduct=1112

Roberts, Wess. Leadership Secrets of Attila the Hun. (1985). Warner Books, Inc.

Sun-Tzu.& Sawyer, Mei-chun. & Sawyer, Ralph D. & Sun Pin. (1996). The complete art of war. Boulder, Colo: Westview Press

Warfare. (n.d.). Dictionary.com Unabridged. Retrieved April 28, 2013, from Dictionary.com website: http://dictionary.reference.com/browse/warfare

http://www.brainyquote.com/quotes/authors/u/ulysses_s_grant.html

http://classic.studylight.org

http://www.merriam-webster.com/dictionary/reconnaissance

Made in the USA
Columbia, SC
23 March 2025